글쓴이 | 박신정

나는 한국의 동해바다의 길 중심에서 창작과
일을 하며 살고 있다.

이 길은 역사가들이나 문화인류학자들이
시베리아에서부터 한국으로 이동한 길이라고
하는 오래전부터 말해온 실크로드의
마지막노선이다.

나의 작업과 관련해서 과거로부터 내려오는
생각과 조형언어에 대해 관심을 갖는 이유는
내가 태어난 곳이 천 년 전에 존재했던
신라왕궁의 유적이 있는 경주라는 도시의
영향이 라고 생각한다.

현대미술을 배우면서도 작가로써 나의
정체성은 이것과 관련함을 느낀다.

무한에 관한 것들에 대한 사람들의 믿음과
철학은 시각형태로 발전되었으며 한민족의
역사 와 자연 환경적 배경과 더불어 형성된
아키타입이 되어있음을 안다.

저자는 이화여대 미술학과와 대학원을
졸업했다. 13년 간의 교수 생활을 마치고
2001년부터 강릉 정동진에서
창작의 길을 걸으며
하슬라아트월드를 만들고 있다.

다른 길, 이 길은 예정된 길이었던가...
A different path. Is this path of mine a predetermined one?

경주에서 강릉까지

From Gyeongju To Gangneung

내 지난 습관과 방황이 영화의 한 장면처럼 보인다

My past habits and wanderings appear like a movie scene.

그리운 평지… 경주

Longing for that lowland…Gyeongju

평지에서 사람들이 술을 마시고 있다
흔들거리는 동작으로 오랫동안 마신다
점점 시끄러워지다가 멈춘다
다시 침묵...

In the field some people are having a drink.
Swinging side to side, they continue drinking.
They are getting louder and soon come to a stop.
Silence again...

"언제 다시 경주로 돌아오세요?"
10년 후… 아니 영원히… 모르겠어… 자신 없이 흐트러진다
미련을 두기에 선택은 그리 호락호락하지 않기에
돌아온다는 여지는 두고 싶지 않았다

"When do you think you will come back to Gyeongju?"
After ten years...no, never...hard to tell...I lose myself at this question.
Since my choice wouldn't accommodate any lingering attachment so easily,
I didn't want to allow myself the possibility of homecoming.

운전하다 갑자기 좁은 시골길로 굽어 들어가는 내가 있다
시골 사람들의 무관심한 시선과 자연조차도
자신을 자랑하지 않는 편안함 때문에
애써 이름 없는 길을 찾아 나선 모양이다

While driving, I sometimes swerve into a narrow country
road impulsively.
Is it the rural people's indifferent gaze or something about
nature that is completely unassuming,
which makes me feel at ease?
Is that why I make the point of seeking a nameless road?

이 길을 가다 보면 무엇을 만날까?
What would I encounter if I continue walking this road?

팻말을 통해서 그나마 유적지임을 알 수 있는 것은
대부분 거대한 무덤들이다

Without the signs you would not know that these
are historical sites,
for they are tombs in the form of gigantic mounds.

무덤의 기록 - 수십 년의 왕의 쟁탈전, 즉위 후 1년 만에 죽다 -
많은 것을 생각했다
우연히 만난 이 무덤 앞에서…
이제 결정을 해야 한다

The records of the tombs--power struggles over several decades and the death within a year after taking the throne.
I thought about many things
in front of this tomb I had stumbled upon...
Now I have to make a decision.

Every week I take a long-distance trip.
So I pack a lot of things like those who go on a long-awaited vacation.
Several extra pairs of clothes, cosmetics and toiletries, and books and a briefcase…
The difference in temperature between Gangneung and Gyeongju could be huge so one must prepare for the unexpected in advance.
If you saw me hitting the road with my three children, you would've thought we were moving house.

나는 매주 긴 여행을 한다
그래서 모처럼의 휴가를 떠나는 사람들처럼 보따리를 많이 들고 다닌다
옷 몇 벌과 세면도구, 화장품, 그리고 책과 서류 가방…강릉과 경주는
기온 차이가 심하기 때문에 예기치 않은 상황에 준비해야 하는 옷과
물건들도 미리 준비해야 한다
특히 내 세 아이와 함께 떠날 때는 자취생 이삿짐 정도는 돼 보인다

The long walk last night is still lingering before my eyes.
From Mangyang that vast sea started showing itself.
It stopped...
A sense of longing is overpowering me,
but why and for what I cannot answer.
It's more like the feeling you get when you throw yourself at life.
Perhaps something you can do little about.
Once you get past the hills of Mangyang, such a conflicted
feeling falls into the subconscious.

간밤의 긴 행보가 아직 눈앞에 어른거린다
망양에서부터 그 큰 바다는 자태를 드러내고 있었다
멈추었다…
그리움이 밀려오지만
왜 무엇을 위한 이유는 찾을 수가 없었다
삶을 향해 던질 때 오는 감정일 것이다
어쩔 수 없는 것이겠지…
망양 고개를 지나면 그런 갈등은 잠재의식 속으로 들어간다

This is Gangneung.

"What time did you arrive?"
"I arrived at dawn."
I hear some intermittent sawing sounds from a workshop nearby.

This place is deep in the mountains.
My longing or even memory of the lowland is disallowed by the overpowering force of the wind.

A blizzard again.
The wind is driving the snow inland from the sea.
Thick snowflakes falling diagonally without a pause...
When will it let up...

The winter here is long.
Just when you think the spring is around the corner, it gets cold and snowy again, so you take your winter clothes out and move around like a sloth.
Curled up in your freezing state, you realize the day has already gone by.
No time even to be distracted by idle thoughts. Then the night comes.

이곳은 강릉

"몇 시에 도착하셨어요?"
"새벽에 도착했어요."
조금 떨어진 작업장에서 톱 소리가 간간이 들린다

이곳은 산속이다
평지에 대한 그리움이나 기억도 여기의 바람 센 기운은 용납하지 않는다

또 폭설.
바람이 바다에서부터 눈바람이 몰려오고 있다
멎음 없이 사선을 그으며 떨어지는 굵은 눈발…
언제 그치려나…

이곳의 겨울은 길다
봄이 오려나 했는데 다시 눈발이 날리며 추워져 다시 두툼한 옷을 꺼내 입고 둔한 동작으로 움직인다
추워 웅크리고 있다 보면 하루는 너무 빨리 없어져 버리고 만다
잡다한 상념에 시달릴 새도 없이 밤이 온다

경주를 생각한다
Thinking about Gyeongju

눈앞에 펼쳐지는 것은 평온한 들판이다 비어있었다
영혼이 과거를 회상하듯 느리게 천천히 한 지점에서 빙빙 둘러본다
그 들판엔 아직 아무도 없다
등장인물을 세우고 싶지만 좀처럼 나타나지 않는다

Before me opens out a silent field. It looks empty.
I take my time looking all around me as if to wait for my soul to bring back the past. I feel like being on a slow merry-go-round.
There is no one yet in that field.
I try to call up the protagonist, but she barely answers.

From the distance a man, apparently on his early morning walk, fast approaches towards me with a towel in his hand. Some time later a man and woman riding a bicycle together make an entrance.
And way over there where a group of foundation stones have been collected I see me and my children treading on them. Once you go around the pagoda that soars to the sky I see some rock art at the foot of a mountain.

멀리서 한 아저씨가 이른 아침 산책을 하는지
한 손엔 수건을 들고 빠른 걸음으로 오고 있는 것이 보인다
한참 후에 자전거를 함께 탄 남녀가 나타난다
그리고 바로 멀리에 모아둔 주춧돌 위를 아이들과 걸어 다니는
내가 보인다. 하늘을 향해 높이 솟아 있는 탑을 돌아 산기슭의
암각화도 보인다

I try to conjure up Gyeongju's winter scenes, but they remain unarticulated.
I see people moving slowly. Rarely any sign of crowdedness.
You can say the same thing about the early spring or the late autumn,
not to mention the wearisome summer.

경주의 겨울을 떠올려 보지만 그려지지 않고 있다
사람들은 느리게 움직이고 있고 붐빔은 거의 없다
상황은 초봄 혹은 늦가을
지루한 여름도 어울린다

For Gyeongju people
a thousand years aren't that far.

When they talk about the past, I mean the distant past,
they reach as far back as a thousand years.
No matter how well-informed they may be about their history,
each and every household has in their possession at least one
old roof tile or a piece of ancient earthenware
found often while building a house...
Once in a while you hear some people even saying that they
saw a gold crown emerging from the ground.

경주 사람들
그들에게 천년은 멀지 않다

사람들은 과거 그것도 아주 오래된
천년의 시간도 이야기한다
역사에 대해 이해하는 이든 아니든
집집마다 오래된 기와장이나 토기 하나쯤은 갖고 있다
집을 짓다가 나왔다든가...
심지어 금관까지도 땅속에서 나온 것을 보았다는 사람들도 간혹 있다

Many of those who were born in Gyeongju grow up playing around the ancient cultural relics.
Looking at my childhood photos, I find most of them taken...
in front of the gigantic royal tombs... while ice-skating at Anapji Pond...
on top of the Cheomseongdae observatory...
These remains from a thousand years ago served as an awesome playground for us.

경주에 태어난 많은 사람들은 문화의 흔적에서 놀이하며 자란다
나의 어린 시절 대부분의 사진들…
거대한 왕의 무덤 앞에서… 안압지에서 스케이트 타며…
첨성대 위에 올라가…
천 년 전의 흔적들은 어린 우리들에게 좋은 놀이터로 제공되었다

The traces of a thousand years,
my childhood playground.

Three siblings in my family,
three siblings in my aunt's family,
these little siblings came together.

In the photo of the tomb the top is
unseen.

천년의 흔적들이 제공하는
어린 시절의 놀이터

우리집 형제 셋
고모집 형제 셋
어린 형제들끼리 모였다

사진 속 무덤엔 꼭대기가 보이지 않는다

그 많은 해도 지나가고
셀 수도 없는 시간도 지나갔다

신라의 유적들은 대부분 파손되고 사라지고
좋았던지 나빴던지도 모르는
역사라는 풍파의 세월

A great number of years passed,
So did the countless hours.

Most of the remains of Silla have been
destroyed or disappeared,
Hard to say whether they were good or
bad,
those stormy years called history.

찬란했던 수도의 중심 유적지 위로
기차가 지나가고 도로가 뚫렸다
힘든 시간을 살아내야 했던 사람들은
과거 유물을 주춧돌 삼아 집을 짓고 살았다

Right through the central historical sites of
the glorious capital
the rail tracks and the motorway now run.
Those who had to endure the hard times
built their houses using the past remains as
their foundation stones.

The thatched houses chaotically scattered on the grounds of
Hwangnyongsa Temple, some of which were my school friends'
homes, were all pulled down one day,
and rebuilt in a standardized section elsewhere.

If the thousand-year relics were toys for us children,
they were no more than a nuisance for the adults who had to make
a living.

황룡사 들판에서 어지럽게 초가를 이루고 살던
친구들의 집들은 어느 날 철거되어
획일한 구획 속에 재배치 되었다

천년의 세월은 어린 시절 아이들의 장난감이었지만
삶을 이끌어야만 하는 어른들에겐 귀찮은 존재 정도였다

A prey is lying in a field,
a muscular body with a horn or a comb.

The delicious and favored parts are all gone,
the last remains and bones are left behind.
.....
I cast my eyes over the fields of Hwangnyongsa.

Only the stone pieces and foundation stones,
things too heavy to carry, remain.

먹잇감이 들에 누워있다
근육질 몸통과 머리에는 뿔인지 벼슬인지를 둘렀다

맛있고 좋은 부위는 다 가져가고
마지막 부산물과 뼈만 남아있다

……

황룡사 들판을 본다

무거워서 가져가지 못한
돌조각과 주춧돌만 남았다

사연이 있어도
아픔이 있어도

비어있어 좋다
뼈만 남아 더 좋다

Whether it has a story to tell,
whether it hides a pain underneath,

it is good it's empty,
It is even better that only the bones have remained.

One story on top of another,
a tower of imagination is being rebuilt.
. . . . .

The imagination closes its eyes and
swims amidst the void.

Lost in the depths of my memory, the
soul of my dreams
flies away again at the calling of the
wind.

이야기는 이야기를 타고
상상의 탑을 다시 세운다
· · · · ·

상상은 눈을 감고 허공을 헤엄친다

기억 속을 헤매는 꿈속의 영혼은
다시 바람의 부름에 날아가 버린다

고향을 찾았다 . . .
I have found my hometown.

The place where my grandmother lived,
the place where my mother lived,
the place where I was held in their arms or carried on their back.

The old iron gate.
I caress the stained tiles.
Warm, beautiful memory.

Unlike the image in my memory,
I'm shocked to find it so tiny and squalid in real life.

Is that memory of mine right?
Can that small yard to be true?

A place where the grapevines and the roses were planted...

where our shaggy dog rested under the magnolias and the peonies,
our neighbors laughed with us on the wide platform bench,
where more than a hundred people would have gathered together for a party,

could this yard have really been that one?

할머니가 살고
어머니가 살고
내가 안기고 업혀 살았던 곳

낡은 철문
때 묻은 타일들을 쓰다듬는다
따뜻했고 아름다웠던 기억

추억의 그림에 비할 바 안되는
작고 초라한 지금에 놀란다

그 기억이 맞는가
저 조그마한 마당이 맞는가

포도나무가 있었고 장미 넝쿨이 있었던…

목련꽃과 모란꽃 아래 삽살이가 쉬고
넓은 평상에서 이웃들이 함께 웃고
잔치를 하고 백 명 이상은 족히 모였을

그 마당이 맞는가

Against the pitch-black earth,
wearing a gold crown, a gold belt, and a sword, a giant is lying down.

His body already gone a thousand years ago, his soul too flown into the long lost time,

I look for its traces.

Owing to my long familiarity and experience perhaps
I am used to this fading out of existence.

검은 흙 속에서
금관을 쓰고 황금으로 된 허리띠와 칼을 찬
십척 장신이 누워 있다

몸체 사라진지 이미 천년
영혼도 먼 시간으로 가버린지 오래

발자취를 돌아본다

오랫동안 보던 반복된 경험 탓인지
이 소멸에 익숙하다

닭이 울고 알에서 왕이 태어났다는 계림 숲에는 미술반 친구들 보다
나이 많은 우람한 나무가 위치하고 있었고 나무와 그 사이의 한옥과
산이 된 거대한 왕의 무덤들...
그 배경 뒤로 사라지는 나지막한 평지의 풍경은
계림 숲 사생대회 그림에 간직되었다

In the mythological forest of Kyerim where a white rooster crowed and a baby king was born in an egg,
an old, majestic tree stood, and between that tree and a hanok shrine loomed royal tombs as big as a mountain,
and the landscape receding behind it
was preserved in a drawing I submitted for the Kyerim Forest Art Contest.

왕이 살았던 반달 모양의 반월성

숲 우거진 멀리로 사라지는
혼재하는 기억의 중첩들

흩어진 유적지의 석재들 틈 사이
남아있는 흔적들

풍경화의 대상이자 사색의 장소

그런...
자연이 된 시간의 흔적들을 그렸다

The palace-fortress of Banwolseong where kings once ruled,

the intermingled layers of my memories disappearing far beyond the dark forest,

the traces left between the gaps of the stones scattered about among the ruins,

the object of my landscape paintings and the place of my contemplation,

Such traces of time...
that which became part of nature I painted.

In a mythological homeland
there exists a destination
where one rests.

There is a time for you to come home
when the harsh winds of the world blow.

신화 속 고향에
휴식하는 사람
정착지가 있다

세상의 거친 바람이 불면
돌아올 때가 있다

인간이 만든 것이
자연이 되기까지
예술이 되기까지

Until what humans make
becomes nature,
until that becomes art.

고즈넉한 경주 평지에
거친 대관령 바람이
불어온다

경주와 강릉...
같으면서도 다른 이야기...

Over the serene lowland of Gyeongju
comes blowing
the wild wind of Daegwallyeong.

Gyeongju and Gangneung...
a similar but different story...

My husband is a strong swimmer.

Beginning in the river Namdamecheon, he would
end up swimming out to the sea.
He grew up making himself at home with both the
river and the sea.

When he got hungry while swimming, he would
grab seaweed or dive for sea urchins and clams.
Born and raised in Gangneung
but calling the rugged mountain village of Wangsan
his ancestral home,
he would forage for wild grapes, gooseberries,
acorns, and chestnuts.

His memories are completely fiFllled with the natural
world of Gangwon Province.

남편은 수영을 잘한다

남대천에서 헤엄치다가 바다로 나아가고
냇가와 바다에 길들여지며 자랐다

헤엄치다 배고프면 미역 따 먹고 잠수해서 성게 조개 잡고
어렸을 적 태어나고 자란 곳인 강릉에서도
병풍 같은 산으로 둘러싸인 산골 왕산이 고향이기에
산속의 머루 다래 열매 식물과 도토리 밤

그의 추억은 온통 강원도의 자연으로 가득 차 있다

For him Gangwon's natural world was a playground and a place of learning.
When I first saw the twisted path high up in the mountains and the snow-covered Gangneung,
they came to me as an object of apprehension as well as that of admiration.
But for those who were born here, that path was a passage of dream linking them to the outside world.

그에게 있어 강원도의 자연은 놀잇거리자 교육장이었고
높은 산 위로 난 꼬부라진 산길과 눈 쌓인 강릉을
처음 대하는 나에겐 두려움이자 감탄의 대상이었지만
이곳이 고향인 그들에게 그 길은
세상 밖으로 이어주는 꿈의 통로였다

Diary of the Women Who Turned Into Tombstones

A recently widowed woman was pulling apart her long cultivated garden as if to punish herself. Moving the heavy stones around here and there, she was pouring out what's left of her feelings of love and hatred while wrestling with the land.

Another woman from the past whose learning and talents came to be celebrated in later times...
Her husband always contradicted her opinion as though he were in a duel with her.
Unbeknownst to others...
it was their way of loving each other.

Yet another woman...
No matter how much she came to be celebrated in history, she never knew it in her short life.
For all her achievements in learning and art she was known only as a good mother.
Her last words that would strike a chord in future mothers:
"Do not remarry."

비석이 된 여인들의 일기

혼자된 한 여인이 그동안 잘 가꾼 자신의 정원을
자해하듯 파헤치고 있다
무거운 돌덩어리를 이리저리 옮기며
남아있는 애증을 땅과 시름하며 쏟아내고 있었다

훗날 칭송받는 학문 높고 재능있는 또 한 여인...
그녀의 의견에 남편은 늘 대결하듯 반대로 행동했다
주변은 알아차리지 못했지만...
그 둘은 전투하며 사랑했다

또 다른 여인...
역사가 아무리 칭송해도 일찍 떠난 그녀는 알지 못한다
학문과 예술에 출중했지만 어머니로만 남았다
어머니들의 스승이 된 그녀의 유언
재혼하지 마세요...

평지의 들을 보며 자란 여자
대관령 산자락 아래 세찬 파도같은 남자
둘은 가끔 힘겨울 때가 있다...

A woman whose temperament grew out of
the lowland,
and a man who grew up in the rough waves
and the mountains of Daegwallyeong,
things can be difficult sometimes between
the two.

상상한 적 없는
사랑에 혼 줄을 놓아버린
젊은 사랑을 본다

죽을 듯 사랑하고
지치도록 미워하는

순서를 바꾸면 인생은 해피엔딩

미워하다 지쳐서
사랑하다 죽는 것으로…

At the undreamt
love two young lovers
let go of themselves.

Loving like crazy,
hating until exhausted.

It's a happy ending in
reverse order.

Shall we say they get tired
of hating
and die loving?

강릉 풍경
Gangneung's landscape

옛사람에게 그림은
창호지 문밖으로 펼쳐진 앞산
호박 넝쿨 올라간 돌담 위로 솟아 있는 하늘

사각 프레임 캔퍼스 액자
그 속에 담으면
그림이 된다

물이 흐르고
언덕은 구비구비
물 강 , 언덕 릉
산수화 같은 곳에 자리 잡았다

In the olden days a picture was a mountain framed
by an open papered window or a sky rising above
the stone wall covered with pumpkin vines.

If you put it on the canvas
and have it framed,
there you have a picture.

Water flowing, hills meandering,
Gang: river, Neung: hills.
It is a place like a literati landscape painting.

돌과 풀꽃으로 덮여 있는 낮은 담들과 큰 소나무의
이야기
잘 버무려진 산나물밥과 같이
자연으로 어우러져 있고

동네 곳곳에 있는 당집들과 세월을 이긴 풍경들
그들의 원시적 냄새와 맛이 어우러져
회자되고 있었다

비빔밥 위의 계란 후라이같이
첨삭된 화룡점정
주술적 이야기 ...

The magical stories about the stone walls covered
with grass fiowers and the Big Pine Tree, like a rice
dish well mixed with mountain vegetables,
taken granted as part of nature,
being faithful to their primitive smell and taste,

were being circulated in various shrines across the
village against the landscape of having beaten the
years.

A magical story without the finishing touch like a
sunny side up egg in a bibimbap.

불교나 유교 이전의 다듬어지지 않은 원초적 형태의 신앙이었던 만큼 그들의 욕구는 단순하게 드러나 있었고 인간의 이성으로 꾸미기 이전의 산신이라든지 해신 같은 것이 대관령 국사성황당이나 단오제 이야기에 녹아 있었다

This folk religion is an unrefined, primitive form of faith predating Buddhism and Confucianism, so you find people's hopes and aspirations plainly exposed in it and such mythological stories involving mountain gods and sea gods that defy human reason are reflected in Daegwallyeong Guksadang Shrine or Gangneung Dano Festival.

푸른 바다의 길 영덕

저곳에 바다가 있다
어지러운 전봇줄과 도로 넘어 산 너머

어설프게 개발된 도로 위를
흙먼지 날리며 거침없는 트럭들이 지나가고

그래도 석양의 색이 독특하다고 생각했는데

넓게 펼쳐진 보랏빛 석양 뒤
그 너머가 바다였다

Youngdeok, a Gateway to the Blue Sea.

Over there is the sea beyond the chaotic power lines and the roads, beyond the mountains.

On the haphazardly paved road defiant trucks go flying kicking up dust.

Still I thought the color of the sunset distinctive.

Behind the purplish glow spreading everywhere, beyond that was the sea.

뒤엉킨 오선지 너머
바다가 들려온다

Beyond the jumbled music sheet
I hear the sound of the sea.

산다는 것이 아무것도 아니게 느껴질 때도 있는데
무명이 된다는 것에 몸서리치며 아파하다가도
차라리 원시의 바보가 될 수 있다는 맹목적인 포기가
짧은 웃음을 지으며
내 빰을 스치고 간다

Sometimes I feel that life is nothing, though
becoming anonymous can be shudderingly
painful.
The thought of surrendering unconditionally to
my becoming a primitive fool brushes against
my cheek with a momentary grin.
v

달리고 달리고 달리고

세 아이를 태우고 다섯 시간가량의 운전으로
겨우 다가간 남편의 곳 강릉

이 열열한 행보 뒤에
한 인간의 자아가 엄마를 벗어나 있었다

Driving On and On and On

After more than five hours of driving with three children on board I finally approach Gangneung, my husband's place.

For this gallant trip one person's ego was found to have freed itself from motherhood.

부조화의 거친 사중주
A Rowdy Quartet in Disharmony

10살 8살 4살의 아이들은 차례대로 한 번씩 부딪쳐서 울고
싸워서 울고
그때마다 꼬불 길을 운전하던 신경 날카로운 엄마는 소리친다
한참 후 큰애 둘은 잠에 떨어지고
4살짜리 막내는 엄마와 함께 음악을 들으며 언니 오빠가 없는
사이에 큰애 흉내를 내며
여러 말을 던진다

The ten-year old, the eight-year old, and the four-year
old, they take turns pushing against each other and
crying, fighting with each other and crying,
Each time they do that, the already nervous mom from
negotiating the winding road bellows.
After a while two older ones fall asleep and the
youngest, while listening to the music from the car
stereo, mimics her eldest.
She then talks to her mom:

지금이 8시 반이에요 …
시계도 볼 줄 모르면서
언제 도착해요…목적지도 모르면서
혼자 몽상하고 혼자 흥얼거리며
좋아하는 음악을 함께 좋아하는 아이에게
내 모습이 있었다

"It's 8:30 now."
But she has yet to learn how to read time.
"When do we arrive?"
But she has no idea of our destination.
Dreaming on her own, humming on her own, taking delight in the music we liked, in such a child I found my own image.

평지의 추억
Memories of the Lowland

갈아놓은 논밭 위에 드리운 저녁노을 더욱 붉은 황토 빛으로 물들인다
평소에도 가끔 그 길을 산책하곤 했지만 석양 때문인지 느낌이 달랐다
길 한가운데 차를 세우고 논밭 가운데 서 본다

메마른 논두렁 날렵하게 생긴 새는
주변을 계속 두리번거리면서도
그 자리에서 움직이지 않는다
나도 고개를 돌려 주변을 보았다

나는 들판 가운데 서 있었고
다시 돌아보니 새는 날아가고 없었다
나도 돌아섰다

The evening sunlight was setting the red, turned-over rice paddies even redder.
Every so often I would come here for a walk, but there was something different that day perhaps because of the sunset glow.
I stopped the car in the middle of the road and got out.

A sharp-looking bird sitting on the parched ridge between the paddies kept looking around without budging.
I too looked around.

I was standing in the middle of the field.
I looked back and the bird was gone.
I too turned back.

다시 아침

아침까지 이어지는 생생한 감정…
그동안 애써왔던 것들에 대한
또 다른 대안으로 어리석게 무엇을 찾지 않겠다는 것

결심한다고 되는 게 아닌데 말이다

Morning Again

The vivid feeling that continues…
about what I've striven for
or how I would not look for something else as an
alternative foolishly.

Not that I would succeed just because I made up my
mind.

일 년 전에 찾아뵈었던 박신정입니다
그래요…

이것은 금은화 나무입니다
향기를 맡아보세요. 얼마나 은은한지.
아침에 깨어 일어나 이 향을 맡지요.
나는 이 넝쿨 아래에서 햇살 가득한 진평왕릉을 바라봅니다

I'm Park Shinjung. I came to see you a year ago.
Yes, I remember.

This is golden-and-silver honeysuckle.
Smell the scent and see how subtle it is.
When I get up in the morning, I smell this scent.
Under this vine I admire the sun-splashed royal tomb
of Jinpyeong.

There is a woman who lives like a recluse at the foot of Nangsan
seen across the meadow from the royal tomb,
but nobody knows this.

Father and daughter.
The tomb of Queen Regnant Seondeok is not very far.

Where would be good?
Near the rotary of Palwujeong... Inwang... in the vicinity of
Hwangnam, where there are many tombs...

Brushing aside all the best places to lay the foundation stones,

in favor of Nangsan out there,
across the meadow of Bomun,

she built it to be near her father.

왕릉에서 저 들판 멀리 보이는 낭산 언저리에 숨은 듯 사는 여자가 있는데
아무도 그녀가 살고 있는지 모른다

아버지와 딸
선덕여왕릉은 멀지 않은 곳에 있었다

어디가 좋을까?
팔우정 로터리 부근.. 인왕.. 황남 부근의 무덤 많은 곳...

반석 좋은 곳 다 두고

외곽 낭산
보문 들판

아버지 가까이에 집을 지었다

정동진
The Seaside Town of Jeongdongjin

결혼 후 경주라는 다른 장소의 기후와 풍경에
감탄하던 나를 남편은 이러저리 데려 다녔다 그때
절벽에서 떨어지는 해안선 위로 난 비포장 길을
한참 가다 만난 초라한 겨울의 기차역과 휘몰아치는
파도와 추위를 나는 기억하고 있다

After my wedding, I went ooh and aah at the climate and scenery of a place so different from mine, so my husband started showing me around. I still remember at the time traveling a road built along the cliff-plunging coastline and encountering a miserable winter train station as well as the whipping sea and the freezing cold.

이곳엔 산신령이 있다
호랑이도 있고 머리 감던 처녀도 있다
신령이 머물만한 산의 비경은 앞마당에서 멀지 않다

This place has mountain spirits,
also tigers and young girls who used to wash their
hair here.The great mountain view bewitching
enough for spirits to stay isn't too far from my
front yard.

바람의 시
The Wind Poem

강릉에 바람이 분다

한밤 중 네모진 캄캄한 방
집 앞 숲에 부는 바람 소리

나를 깨웠다

모두들 잠에 들어 혼자 듣는 저 소리
남편을 깨우지만
귀찮은 듯 고개 돌린다

소나무 땜에 그래

온통 캄캄한 산속의 방
그 안에서 나는 뜬눈으로 있었다

바람 땜에 그래

오늘도 바람이 분다
바람은 숲속의 나무와 땅을 말리고
주변의 것들을 다 마르게 하고 있지만
젖어 들고 있는 그 무언가가 있다

The wind is blowing in Gangneung.

In the dead of night, in the dark square room, the sound of the wind from the forest in front of the house

woke me up.

All asleep, I alone listen to that sound.

I try to wake up my husband, but he turns aside as if irritated,

"It's the pines."

In the mountain room as black as pitch, in that space I was wide awake,

"It's the wind."

The wind is blowing again today.

It dries the trees and the soil and everything else around, but there is something that soaks its way in.

소나무 땜에 그래
바람 땜에 그래

It's the pines.
It's the wind.

The seaside road, the sea cliffs,
the dark sea below,
no way of telling how deep it is.

The night has hidden the sea movements
in its dark silence, and its own feelings.

The motion. The sound of waves.
Slowly, slowly.

해안 길 바다 절벽
그 아래 검은 바다
깊이를 알 수 없다

밤은 바다의 움직임을 검은 침묵 속에 감춰버리고
자신의 감정 또한 숨겨 버렸다

움 직 임 파 도 소 리
천 천 히   천 천 히

검은색 그라데이션
어둠 속 바다

내 코앞에 있을 듯한 무엇도 보이지 않는다

The gradients of the color black,
the sea in the dark.

There may be something before me,
I cannot see anything.

흑암 같은 먹먹한 속
검은 파도의 아우성

앞에 있을 것 같고
아주 가까이에 느껴지는 무엇

손을 내저으며
한 발자국씩 발을 딛는다

말 없는 침묵에게 손을 내민다

Being inside as dark as a melanocratic rock,
howling of the black sea.

Something might be before me,
something I can feel very close to me.

Waving my hand side to side,
I inch forward little by little.

I offer my hand to the speechless silence.

At first glance my path appeared to have stopped and changed direction, but I don't think it stopped at that point in time.I think it was a matter of taking a different means and angle.
It looked as if I stopped what I had been doing,
but I was looking at my work and myself objectively.

There were two paths to choose from: the beaten one and the unbeaten one.
The former is what someone else has chosen before you, whereas the latter is what no one else has.
It is about casting your lot with the unknown.
I chose the latter.

그렇게 겉으로 보았을 땐 내 길이 멈춘 것처럼 다른 방향으로 간 것처럼 보였다
그러나 그 시점에서 내가 멈춰있었던 건 아니고
방식과 각도를 달리한 것이라 생각한다
하던 일을 멈춘 것처럼 보였지만 나는 내 일과
나 자신을 냉정하게 보고 있었다

길이 보이는 것과 길이 보이지 않는 것에 있어서
길이 보이는 것은 이미 누군가 그 길을 가 버린 것에 해당하고
길이 보이지 않는다는 것은 아무도 가지 않은
새로움에 도전하는 일이다
어쨌든 이 길은 내 인생에 있어서 보이지 않는 길을 가는 것에 해당한다

다른 길...
이 길은 예정된
길이었던가...

A different path...
Is this path
a predetermined one?

길이 보이지 않는다
길을 낸다
길을 간다

I cannot see my path ahead.
I make my own path.
I go on that path.

When a cold sea wind assails the pines,
a beautiful mist of tears rises in their midst.

The shoulder heavily burdened with rocks
and the dropping head from behind.

....
I was unable to offer any words of consolation.
I knew laying them down was nothing,
but I was unable to say so.

차가운 해풍이 소나무에 불어오면
그곳에 일렁이는 아름다운 눈물 안개

바위를 잔뜩 올린 어깨에
고개 숙인 뒷모습

....

위로의 말을 건넬 수가 없었다
내려놓음은 아무것도 아님을 아는 것인데
말하지 못했다

On the Way to Temple Yongyeonsa

I left home
to come here.

The road comes to a stop at the foot of a cliff.
On the way to Temple Yongyeonsa beyond Sacheon Reservoir.
Ah, I'm glad I'm here.

I get myself together and start an uphill climb.
I'm glad I'm here.

On the way to Temple Yongyeonsa beyond Sacheon Reservoir.

The lone mountain that sticks out roundly
and that pine tree to complete the picture. A mountain stream
spirals down dizzily.

Ah, I'm glad I came here alone.

A gush of feeling inside of me.
Why am I like this?

Perhaps
here
a pair of spirits
dwell here.

I gather myself together and continue climbing.
A little memorial stone by the road.

Our departed so and so,
may its spirit...

Ah, why am I crying
before this unknown stone?

용연사 가는 길

나는 떠나왔고
이곳에 왔다

가다 말고 멈춰 선 벼랑길
사천 저수지 너머 용연사 가는 길
아! 내가 이곳에 오길 잘했구나.

감정을 추스르고 숨고르는 오르막길.....
내가 이곳에 오길 잘했구나...

사천 저수지 너머 용연사 가는 길

둥글게 홀로 튀어나온 산과
어우러진 저 소나무
어지럽게 휘감으며 내려치는 물

아! 홀로 이곳에 오길 잘했구나.

솟아오르는 감정
내가 왜 이러나!
이곳에서

아마도
한 쌍의 혼령이
이곳에 머무르나 보다

감정을 추스르고 오르는 오르막길
그 아래 작은 추모비

불귀의 우리○○
부디○○ .. 하소서 라고

아! 내가 왜 눈물 흘리나!
모르는 비석 앞에서

It's been snowing all day.
When the accumulation exceeds one meter, we scramble to prevent our workshop from collapsing.
The road was impassable so none of our workers could make it nor could we expect any help with the snow.
Me and my assistant Jihee are at panic stations.
We try throwing a rope over and start swinging it wildly to get the snow off the roof.
An inexperienced southerner such as myself is not being a big help for things like this.

Then it occurs to me, Ah, so here I am...
I who ended up in these rugged mountains,
I who crossed into this completely different world,
It is at this person I found myself surprised.

하루 종일 눈이 그치지 않는다
계속 오는 눈이 1미터를 넘어가자 작업장이 넘어간다고 난리다
길이 불통되어 작업장 식구들은 출근도 못 하고 눈을 치울 사람도 없다
나와 나의 작업을 도우려고 온 지희는 안절부절이다
밧줄을 지붕 너머로 보내 휘두르면서 눈을 지붕에서 떨어뜨렸다
일할 줄도 모르는 남쪽 나라에서 온 내가 이런 일에 별로 도움이 되지 않고 있다

문득 아! 내가 여기에 살고 있구나 하는 느낌…
이 산속까지 와 버린 나에게
상당히 다른 곳에 와 버린 나에게
스스로 놀라고 있었다

He saw the snow rolling in from the sea and predicted it would be a heavy snowfall.
Work goes well when you're in sync, and my husband grumbled that a clumsy worker wasn't much help, yet he seemed to be enjoying the situation and handled it skillfully.

I was usually the one who caused problems in these situations. At times like that, my husband would scold me like a boss reprimanding a dull-witted private, or he would play a trick on me.
Once, he seriously advised me that if I wrapped my feet in plastic bags while wearing my shoes, the water wouldn't get in, as he was worried about my shoes getting wet from the snow.
I believed and followed his advice, but I ended up slipping and sliding around the whole time.

눈이 바다 쪽에서부터 밀려오는 걸 보더니 폭설일 거라고 남편은
예언한다
일도 손발이 맞아야 잘되는 법...어둔한 일꾼이 별로 도움이 안 된다고
푸념하면서도 남편은 이 상황을 즐기는 것 같았고 능숙하게 대처했다

이 상황에서 문제를 일으키거나 하는 사람은 주로 나였다
그럴 때면 남편은 덜떨어진 졸병을 혼내는 상사처럼 나를 나무라거나
아니면 나에게 장난을 치곤 했다 한번은 눈에 내 신발이 젖는 것을
염려하며 신발을 신은 채로 비닐봉지로 내 발을 감싸면 신발에 물이
들어가지 않는다고 진지하게 충고했다
그래서 믿고 따르다가 계속 미끄러지며 다닌 적이 있다

살을 에는 추위에 결혼 초 5년 동안은 강릉에 오기만 하면 아파 누웠다
차디찬 추위만큼이나 센 말투는 나를 당혹하게 할 때가 많았으며 음식 또한 잘 맞지 않았다
조용하게 눈을 즐기고 모든 것을 흰색으로 지워버린 눈 속의 고립을 즐기기엔
모든 것이 불편한 현실이었고 소란하기만 했다

Unable to cope with the freezing weather of Gangneung, for the first five years I got sick every time I came here.
The local dialect as strong as the cold weather threw me off many a time, and the food didn't agree with me either. To be able to quietly enjoy the snow that buried everything in white and the isolation it provided, everything was too inconvenient and discordant.

그렇지만 눈 속의 세 아이와 우리는 그 속에서 생동하는 자연을 느끼고 있었고 입으로 이곳의 아름다움을 칭찬하지 않았지만... 그러나 나는 아직도 그 겨울의 하얗게 얼어버린 오봉댐과 소나무를 깊이 뒤덮은 눈들을 잊을 수가 없다

아!
나는 신선의 풍경을 보았다

But in that snow me and my three children were feeling the natural world vibrant with life, even if we weren't exactly praising it in words. I still cannot forget the Obong Dam frozen white and all the snow on top of the pine trees in that winter.

Ah,
I saw a landscape of Taoist immortals.

The Making of Haslla

This mountain standing high above the sea,
how did it meet the ledge of the Jeongdongjin
coastline?

It was a path I had to follow.
It was a project I had to do.

To make something, a habit ingrained in my body
going back to my major...

I needed work, whether of art or of everyday life.

The contingent becoming the necessary,
a habit ingrained in my body,

the making of Haslla Art World.

하슬라 꾸미기

바다 위에 우뚝 선 이 산
어떻게 해서 이곳 정동진 바다 기슭의 산을 만나게 되었을까?

필연적으로 가야만 되는 길이고
해야만 하는 일이었다

나의 전공에서 시작된 내 몸의 습관이 되어버린 무엇인가를
만드는 것...
예술이든 일상의 일이든 일감이 필요했다

우연이 필연이 되는
내 몸의 습관

하슬라아트월드 만들기

I looked and searched everywhere, so many times.
If I liked something, something else got in the way.
Kept looking here and there...

Then I found this place,
the place that has both the mountains and the sea.
There was no other choice to consider.

This was it.

많이도 구하고 헤매었던
마음에 들면 인연이 닿지 않고
이리저리 ...

그러다가 만난 이곳
바다와 산을 함께 가진 곳
선택의 여지가 없었다

이곳이다

Our home where we lived and played with three children suddenly disappeared into the downpour of Typhoon Rusa.

The day the flood damage was inflicted we were there till the end.

The space filled with the energy of artworks was gone and turned into a desolate place buried by an avalanche of rocks.

Typhoon Rusa moved the mountains.
Everything became strange and disjointed, and we were thrown back to the wilds of Gangwon-do, to its beginnings.

Huge rocks fallen from the mountains blocked the roads, beautiful pine trees lost their balance and fell upon their broken limbs, and the roads splintered like in an earthquake and were gone.

After a long night, the morning came when the rain stopped.
A limpid sunlight shone as if to penetrate through the skin, and clear streams of water were overflowing everywhere.

The kids, having already forgotten the terror of the past two days, jumped into the clear water and played with their new toys.

What Goddess Rusa showed
in her last concert was bright and serene.

미스 루사
Miss Rusa

아이들과 함께 뛰어놀고 생활하던 우리 집이
루사 태풍 물속에 사라졌다

수해가 나는 날 우리는 끝까지 그곳에 있었다

작품에 의해 공간의 에너지를 채우던 그 공간은 없어지고
거친 바위들로 가득한 황량한 곳이 되어버렸다

루사 태풍은 산을 옮겨 놓았다
모든 것은 달라졌고 불통 되어
야생의 강원도, 그 태초에 우리를 있게 하였다

산에서 내려온 산만한 돌은 도로를 가로막고 있었고
멋진 소나무들은 제 균형을 잃고 부러진 채 넘어져
도로는 지진 난 것처럼 갈라져 사라졌다

긴 밤을 지나
비가 그친 아침
태풍 이후 투명한 햇빛은 피부를 뚫을 듯했고
곳곳에서 맑은 물이 흘러넘쳤다

아이들은 이틀 동안 겪은 공포도 잊고
맑은 물속에 들어가 새로운 놀잇감을 만지며 즐겁게 노는 것이다

.....

루사 여신이 보여준
연주의 마지막은 밝고 고요했다

In my memory I can trace my own room.

The door chimed when I opened it.
One of the walls was completely covered with books.
Old letters and albums, slides, academic papers, discs, CDs, and video tapes, these were neatly stacked on the floor.

My rectangular room had, against its narrower wall,
a cabinet just right in size where I kept my favorite and secretive things.

From all my personal records including the fragments from my past journeys to my photos and appointment book clippings, books written by my favorite authors, on feminism, surrealist art, and the personal letters I couldn't part with as well as the ones I did not send...

There were many things I could not throw away.

기억의 방
The Room of Memories

기억 속에서도 내 방을 더듬을 수 있다

문을 열면 딸랑이는 방울 소리가 나고
벽면 전체는 가득한 책이 있고
오랜 편지 자료들과 앨범
슬라이드, 논문, 디스켓, CD, 비디오 자료들
이것들은 바닥에서부터 가지런히 쌓아 올려두었다

직사각형으로 생긴
내 방 좁은 한 벽면엔
딱 알맞은 크기와 높이의 장롱이 있었는데
그 안엔 나의 애장품들이 들어 있었고
비밀스러운 것들도 그 안에 들어 있었다

내 기록의 모든 것과 내 지난 여정에서 만난 부스러기부터
사진 그리고 스크랩된 일정들까지
좋아하는 작가들의 책
페미니즘
초현실주의 미술 서적들
그리고 버리지 못하는 편지들…
보내지 않은 편지들…

버리지 못하는 것들이 많았다

The outdoor sculpture in a lawn that I couldn't possibly imagine now, the images of the past that I have filled out diligently.

Would the expression "emptied out" be right?
Or "It went back to where it belongs"?
What I do not remember...what are they and how many of them... and what I do remember...where have they gone...

I did not blame nature
that had reverted things back to nothing.

Instead I tried to find the reason
within myself.

지금은 상상이 안 되는 야외 조각과 잔디밭
열심히 채워왔던 과거의 모습들

비어버렸다는 표현이 맞을까?
옛날의 제자리로 되돌아갔다는 표현이 맞을까?
기억나지 않는 것들이 무엇이며 몇 개인지…
그리고 기억에 있는 것들은 어디에 가 있는지…

아무것도 아닌 것으로 되돌려 버린 자연에게
이 상황을 탓하지도 않았다

이 상황의 이유에 대해
나로부터의 이유를 찾으려고 했다

정동진
옛 그대로의 바다 자태

불 밝음 등명이라는 지명
해가 아름답게 떠오른다

Jeongdongjin
A look of the sea the way it has always been.

The name Deungmyeong,
lantern offered to spirits and the Buddha.
The sun rises beautifully.

Heavy with a knotted heart
after I quit what I had been doing
and went off to somewhere,
the radiant sea was untying that knot for me.

하던 일을 그만두고
어딘가로 떠난 마음의 매듭을
밝은 바다가 푸르게 풀어주고 있었다

Working on a Land Art Project

But people often asked why I did such a work.
Same with what I am trying to do now.

Question marks of incomprehensibility
thrown about me...

대지 공간 작업

그러나 가끔 사람들은 왜 그 일을 하느냐고 물었다
지금 내가 시도하는 일에 대해서도 그렇다

그렇게 내 주위에 던져지는
의아함의 의문부호들....

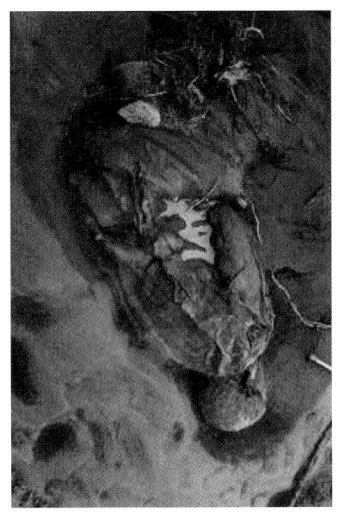

Sometimes you get
paper cuts that hurt.

I had no time or energy
to set right what people were saying.

My poor social skills
would only make things worse.

At the pounding of my heart
the logic of explanation lost its order.

Things I was unable to ignore,
things not so important after all,

those cuts under my nails
lasted a long time...

때론 종이에도
손가락이 베이듯

사람들의 말에
바로잡을 시간도 힘도 없었다

나의 서툰 사회성은
정신없는 행동만 할 뿐

심장의 두근거림에
해명할 논리는 순서를 잃었다

내려놓지 못한 것
별것 아닌 것

손톱 밑의 작은 상처
오래갔다 ...

나의 이상적 아름다움
My Ideal Beauty

자연을 더욱 자연스럽게
예술도 너무 큰 목소릴 내길 원치 않는다

To make nature more natural.
Art too does not want to speak too loudly.

공원의 이름을 정해야 한다..
결정했다
과거 신라 때 부르던 강릉의 옛 이름 하슬라

내가 자라온 경주와 연결하려는 의도였을까
실크로드를 따라 힘겹게 이동했을 사람들의 이야기처럼
나라 밖의 사람들과 교류하길 희망함일까?

We have to name the park…
Decided.
Haslla. Gangneung's old name used in Silla.

Was it my intention to link it with my hometown Gyeongju?
Like those adventurous Silk Road travelers' stories,
was it my hope to interact with people from overseas?

들판에 대한 그리움 달래기
Nursing My Longing for the Lowland

돌아가신 친정어머니처럼
경주 들판이 한 번씩 그리울 때

드넓은 들판 강릉 하시동을 간다

서쪽 멀리는 대관령이 있고 동쪽 끝에는 바다가 있다

신라 화랑의 이야기가 여기도 있고
김유신과 차 유적지 한송정도 있지만

그리워하러 간다
…

Like my late mother
when I miss the fields of Gyeongju,

I go out to the wide-open area of Hasi-dong
in Gangneung.

To the west is Daegwallyeong, to the east is the sea.

Here you have Silla stories about the Hwarang
warriors
and Kim Yusin and the tea-drinking site of
Hansongjeong,

but I go there to nurse my longing for the lowland.

When I was a first grader in elementary school, they
took us to Baegyulsa on a school picnic.

This is the place where the martyr Yi Chadon was
beheaded
and shed white blood.

So it was named White Blood Temple,
said our teacher.

I stared at the slightly faded misty rock for a long time,
and climbed the endless stone steps pantingly with
multiple rest stops.

From the cotton candy peddler who followed after
school picnics
I bought a fipple flute with all my allowance money
and gave up that sweet stuff.

하얀 피
White Blood

국민학교 일학년 소풍 장소...백율사!

이차돈이 순교해 그의 목이 떨어지고
흰 피를 쏟았다는 곳

그래서 백율사라고
담임선생님은 설명했다

나의 두 눈은 약간 바랜 희뿌연 바위를 한참이나 쳐다보았고
몇 번이나 쉬며 다리 아프게 올라갔던 높은 돌계단과
아이들 소풍마다 찾아다니는 솜사탕 아이스크림 파는 상인에게서
달콤한 그것 모두를 포기하고 용돈 전부를 마음에 쏙 드는 피리와
바꾸었다

그런 피리를 산꼭대기 사찰 깊은 우물가에 두고 내려와
내내 우울했던 그날의 소풍 기억은
하얀 피와 뒤범벅되어
어린 시절 꾸었던 꿈같이 남아있다

But when I found out I had left the flute by the well in that
mountain-top temple, I was crestfallen all day.
That memory of my school picnic,
jumbled with white blood,
has remained with me like a dream dreamt by my younger self.

동네 전체에 구름처럼 아련했던 하얀 피의 이야기는
산업도로로 변한 대형트럭들의 거친 소리로 메워졌다

그러나 나는 그 길을 지날 때마다
절간에 두고 온 아스라한 피리 소리에 남겨진 그 하얀 피의 신화를 되새긴다

The story about white blood hovering over the whole neighborhood like a cloud got buried by the loud noise of the big trucks running on the new industrial road.

Whenever I pass that road, though,
I can't help thinking about the myth of white blood echoing in the faint sound of the flute I left in the temple.

What sort of sound must have come out of that lost flute?

잃어버린 그 피리에는
어떤 소리가 담겨 있었을까?

Where I was born there were royal tombs as large as a mountain, and we lived right around them.

They were our playground, our battleground.
Today there is a controversy
about some of these mounds,
whether they can be called royal tombs or not...
When my eldest brother in his mid-50s, over drinks with his friends, raised his voice louder than the scholars',
it called up our tangled memories hidden somewhere.

내가 태어난 동네엔 산만한 왕릉들이 있었는데
우린 그 주변에 살았다고 한다

그곳은 아이들의 놀이터이자 싸움터였고
지금에 와서 학술적 논란이 되는
몇몇 개의 능들의 모양에 관해
왕릉이다 아니다..
학자들보다 더 큰 목소리를 내는
50대 중반의 큰오빠 친구들의 술자리 이야기는
어딘가에 숨어있는 뒤엉킨 기억들과 함께한다

The deep water of Yegicheongsu (or Aegicheongso) is as clear as glass.
It flows north from the Seocheon of Gyeongju in a curve.
When you look down at the Gyeongju cityscape from the terrace of Geumjangdae, you can see the flow of the Bukcheon merges with that of the Seocheon creating a whirlpool.

The rock painting was carved on the cliff against which the whirlpool clashes, a picture before the invention of letters, an icon like a cipher.

A sacred place of myths and legends, where no one could get close easily.

극적 분기점의 맑은 물
Clear Water at a Dramatic Intersection

애기청소는 수심이 깊고 맑기가 유리알 같은
경주의 서천에서 북으로 흘러가는 곡선 모양의 맑은 물.......
금장대에서 경주시가지를 내려다보면 북천의 물이
서천의 물과 섞이면서 소용돌이친다

그곳 벼랑에 새겨진 암각화
글자 이전의 그림
암호 같은 도상

신성한 장소로써 신화와 전설을 간직한
물이 깊고 사람이 근접하기 어려운 곳이었다

Have you ever tried diving at Aegicheongso?
I'm sure kids and diving are inseparable in any river town, but this place was notable for the daredevil stories people told about their childish exploits.
Do you know why it's called Aegicheongso?
It's because every year at least one person dies there...
because of the whirlpool where you get trapped...

Such stories have been passed down among the local kids with fear and fascination.

너 애기청소에서 다이빙 해 봤냐?...
어느 동네나 어릴 적 개울가에서 다이빙하며 놀지만
그곳은 어릴 적 무용담을 이야기하는 특별한 장소였다
이름이 왜 애기청소 이냐?
그곳엔 소용돌이가 있어 들어가면 빠져나오지 못한다던가
해마다 한 명씩 죽는다는 등...

이야기는 아이들 사이에 약간의 두려움과 함께 전해졌다

Shadowless Pagoda

The stonemason Asadal who built the Seokgatap pagoda
and his love story with Asanyeo,

according to which the shadow of the pagoda, upon its
completion, must be reflected on the pond Yeongji located
far away.

When Asanyeo threw herself into the pond
after the reflection on the clear surface like the mirror Min
jing, did she really see the shadow of the pagoda?

The shadowless pagoda and the mirror pond.

The pagoda and the pond remain,
but there is still no shadow.

Between the mysterious gap
between the surreal legend and memory
my mind's afterimages were overlapped layer after layer

and became a stone pagoda.

그림자 없는 탑

불국사 석가탑을 만든
석공 아사달과 아사녀의 사랑 이야기

석가탑이 완성되면 멀리 떨어진 영지라는 연못에
탑 그림자가 비쳐야 한다

명경처럼 맑은 물속에 비친 그 …
물속으로 따라간 아사녀는
진정 탑의 그림자를 보았는가?

그림자 없는 탑과 거울 연못

연못과 돌탑은 남아있지만
그림자는 없다

초현실적 전설과 기억의
묘한 간격 사이로
마음의 잔상이 켜켜이 쌓였다 .

돌탑이 되었다

나에겐 이런 것이 있다

과거의 신화 속의 인물에 대한 착각
역사적 서술보다 아사달 아사녀 이야기 속의 예술과 사랑의 현존

물속에 비치는 탑을 기다리는 화두

I have something like this in me.

The illusion about the individuals in a myth of the past, and the coexistence of art and love in the story about Asadal and Asanyeo rather than any historical narrative.

A conversation topic that awaits the pagoda throwing its reflection upon the water.

나의 예술적 주제를 박물관에서 만났다

전생을 보는 거울, 업경
그림자 없는 탑

거울 속에서
그림자 없는 탑이 어른거린다

I met my artistic subjects in a museum.

The mirror that sees one's past life, Eopgyeong.
The shadowless pagoda.

In the mirror
the shadowless pagoda glimmers.

My Gyeongju stories are like
the mirror reflecting my life.

I go for visual pleasuresand the pleasure you get
when you try to share our visual feeling with others.
Cultural artifacts allow you to go beyond nature in a
thrilling way.

That's why I want to share it.
Call it a pleasurable feeling, if you like

I'm attracted to things visual, and I have the habit of
visiting certain places for contemplation and
consolation.

Fragments of memory through the space and time
of a millennium. Even in very trivial things can one
find a genetic puzzle. Time from a thousand years
ago has hidden itself among human traces.

To show Gyeongju is to show my heart.

거울놀이
Playing in the Mirror

경주 이야기는
나의 삶의 거울 같다

나는 시각적인 즐거움을 누리려고 한다
내 시각의 감정을 타인과 공유할 때의 즐거움
문화유적은 자연을 넘어선 탄성을 준다

그래서 나누려고 한다
즐거운 감정이라 해도 된다

나는 시각적 취향을 갖고 있고
공간을 찾아가 생각에 젖거나 위로받는 버릇이 있다

천년 시공 속 기억의 파편들
아주 조그마한 것에도 유전적 퍼즐이 있다
천 년 전의 시간은 인간의 흔적에 숨어있었다

경주를 보여주는 일은 내 마음을 보여주는 것이다

When I show my Gyeongju around,
I think about the time and angle of presentation.

The pond of Anapji is best seen when grasses are still wet in morning dew. The grounds of the Hwangnyongsa are particularly beautiful at sunset. When visiting Bulguksa Temple, I prefer a quiet walk on the back alley through the pine forest. It is a shame it's not open to the public.Should you have foreign visitors, I would urge them to go see the rites of the Bulguksa monks against the tolling of the bell at dawn and the sound of the drums at dusk. They would be moved to tears.

To maximize the leisure of enjoying a cup of tea or coffee, you seek the most aesthetically agreeable taste.
Same with seeing.

Considering that a place gives you a different feeling at a different time, you try to match each place with its best time when you show people around.

나는 경주를 보여줄 때
시간과 각도에 맞추어 보여준다

안압지는 오전 풀잎에 물기가 마르지 않았을 때가 좋고
황룡사의 들판은 역시 황혼이 아름답다
불국사는 가능하다면 송림 우거진 뒷길로 조용히 산책하며 가는
것이 좋지만 일반인에게 개방하지 않는 것이 아쉽다
손님이 외국인이라면 황혼의 법고 소리와 새벽 종소리에 어우러진
불국사 스님들의 예불을 보여주면 눈물을 흘릴 정도가 될 것이다

한잔의 차와 커피도 그 여유를 최고로 하기 위해
가장 탐미적인 맛을 찾듯이 보는 것도 마찬가지다

장소가 시간에 따라 느낌을 달리하고 있는 점에 착안하듯
시시각각 가장 좋은 시간과 가장 좋은 장소를 소개한다

경주, 비어있는 들판의 고요함
강릉, 바다와 대관령의 포효

경주는 돌 속에 침묵하고
강릉은 파도 소리에 운다

Gyeongju, the quietude of an empty field.
Gangneung, the roaring of the sea and Daegwallyong.

Gyeongju is silent inside a stone.
Gangneung is crying at the sound of waves.

Gangneung's landscape is unassertive like a literati painting.

But my Gangneung is
a snow-covered visage of the wind-blasted winter,
a meandering river through the up-and-down mountain terrain,
a cold gust of ocean wind beating at the crooked pines,
and that which contains all those hard years and han (resentful sorrow).

This is Gangneung's landscape painting.

강릉의 풍경
Landscape of Gangneung

산수화에 담긴 강릉의 풍경은 소담하다

그러나 나의 강릉은
바람 부는 겨울 눈 덮인 설경
오르락내리락하는 산세 사이로 굽이치는 강물
휘어진 소나무에 부는 차가운 바닷바람
험한 세월과 한을 고스란히 가진 모습이다

이것이 강릉의 풍경화이다

At first glance Gyeongju and Gangneung,
as old cities, appear to be similar.
Both look for dignity and class, and regard change as burdensome.
Each boasts of famous female personalities:
Queen Seondeok, Nammo and Junjeong of the
Wonhwa organization in the former; and Shin Saimdang
and Heo Nanseolheon in the latter.

But they are very different from each other.

얼핏 보면 경주와 강릉은
오래된 도시로서 서로 비슷해 보인다
품위와 격을 찾고 변화를 어려워한다
여왕과 원화가 있었던 곳이고
신사임당과 허난설헌이 있었던 곳이기도 하다

그러나 아주 다르다

음정으로 치면 저음과 고음에 해당하고
악기로 치면 관악기와 현악기 같은 차이다

경주는 에너지가 숨어있다
강릉은 자연의 에너지가 드러나 있다

If one is a low note, musically speaking,
the other would be a high note;
If one is a string instrument, the other
would be a brass instrument.

In Gyeongju nature's energies are
hidden;
in Gangneung they are exposed.

A stream of water starting from Daegwallyeong becomes a river discharging itself into the East Sea via Gangneung.
So flows the river Namdaecheon right through the city center of Gangneung, which then swerves by Gyeongpo Beach
before meeting the East Sea.

강의 문은 늘 열려있다
The river's gate is never closed.

대관령에서부터 시작된 물은 강이 되어
강릉 동해 바다로 흘러간다
그렇게 남대천은 강릉 시내를 가로질러
경포 옆 강문으로 흘러
동해바다로 흘러가고 있었다

왜
강릉 사람들은 강이 끝나고
바다가 시작되는 곳을
바다의 문이라 부르지 않을까?

Why
don't the locals call
the spot where the sea begins
"the gates of the sea"?

바다가 시작되고
바다의 입구이고
강이 바다를 만나는데

Isn't it where the sea begins,
an entrance to the sea,
where the river meets the sea?

Yes, I got it!

The sea is indeed the river's gate,

the gate through which the river reaches the sea,
the gate through which the river becomes the sea,
River   Gate.

맞았다!

바다는 강의 문이었다

강이 바다로 가는 문
강이 바다가 되는 문
강   문

저 문을 열면 바다가 된다
When you open that gate, it becomes the sea.

강에서
바다로

From the river
to the sea

큰 그릇에
담긴다

in a big vessel
it is contained.

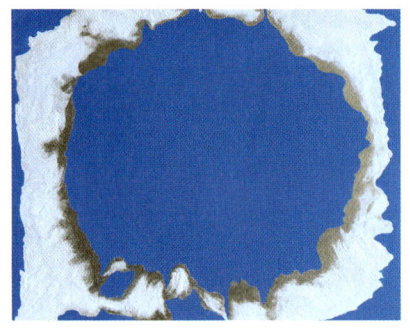

Petals and sprouts,
a breath,
that story.

Your novel,
written in transparent brushstrokes.

Wings light as a ramie jacket,
a butterfly tale like that.

The more you hold the memories,
the lighter they become

flying through the window of time.

꽃잎 새싹
숨결
그 이야기

투명한 붓글씨로 쓴
너의 소설

모시 저고리 가벼운 날개
그런 나비 이야기

기억을 담고 또 담아도
더 가벼워지는 무게

시간의 창을 날아간다

춥지 않고 덥지 않은   Not so cold, not so hot,
바람 좋은   pleasantly breezy,
몇 안 되는 날   on so few a day like this,

눈이 부시는 햇살   in such a dazzling sunlight,
그 빛 한가운데서   basking in that light,
숨을 고르자   let me catch my breath.

항상 그렇듯이   Like always,
그 정원에 나 앉아   go sit in that garden
생각에 잠기자   and lose yourself in thought.

Time passing slowly

The shroud of idle thoughts occupying my mind,
I lift that curtain.

Pushing back the noise from the outside,
I become friends with the silence from the depth of
my heart.

The sea drunk in the setting sun,
the robust mountains,
the life-affirming air,

in that place I sit face to face with me.

천천히 흐르는 시간

모르게 스며드는 상념의 막
그 천을 걷는다

바깥 소리를 뒤로 하고
마음 깊은 침묵과 친구가 된다

노을 깊은 바다
굳건한 산
삶을 보듬는 공기

그곳에서 나와 마주 앉는다

그렇게
종착지

경주에서 강릉
강릉에서 경주 이야기를

여기에 담아 본다

Like that,
my final destination.

From Gyeongju To Gangneung
and from Gangneung To Gyeongju,

that story has been told here.

경주에서 강릉 이야기가
강릉에서 경주로 이어진다
나의 실크로드가 이어진다

From Gyeongju To Gangneung
continues with From Gangneung To Gyeongju.
So my own Silk Road goes on.

작가의 마치는 말

이 글은 시간상으로 일정하게 연속된 이야기가 아니다
이야기들은 시간의 흐름과 관계없이 뒤섞여 있고
기억상실증에 걸려있는 사람이 기억을 더듬는 것처럼 되어있다

순서는 없다
시간과 공간을 함께 느끼기 위해서 그것이 좋을 것 같았다

지난 시간을 적는다는 것이 그 지난 시간을 얼마나 담아낼 수 있을까...

그 시간들은 오히려 나의 글 밖에서 나를 바라보고 있을지 모른다

이 글은 경주와 강릉이라는 아름다운 장소를 중심으로 사색한 이야기며
낯선 곳에 살아가기와 사랑과 꿈이 겹친 것들에 몸으로 부딪쳐서
알 때마다 아팠지만 소중했던 추억의 기록이다

13년을 떨어져 살면서 우리는 매주 경주에서 강릉을 잇는 동해안 길을 왔다
갔다가 했고 그 길에서 많은 생각을 하며 보냈다
작가로서의 나의 길에 상상력과 모태가 된 것은 경주와 강릉의 오랜 도시의
분위기와 자연과 공간이 주는 느낌이었다.

나는 이 길 속에서 갈등한 일과 버림과 선택, 명확함이라는 것 때문에 힘들어하기도 했었다
그 길은 항상 나에게 여러 가지 이야기를 하고 있었고 7번 국도 경주에서 강릉으로 이어지는 긴 여정에서 내 이야기를 들어주고 있었다

미루고 미루었던 일이었다
시작한다고 선언했지만
게으르게 추진하고 있는 자신을 본다

느리고 생각이 많고
얽매여 있었던 많은 것들
가정, 교육, 규범, 시선, 성공...
항상 자유롭지 않다고 생각하며 살았다

이상은 다른 곳에 있다는 생각과
사회생활로써 사람들과의 만남은 늘 어색했다
그 대신 혼자서 작품을 만드는 것이나
내가 좋아하는 공간에서 한참을 앉아있거나
먼 길도 마다하지 않고 찾아간 산길을 무심히 걷는 것이나
들판을 걷는 것과 도시를 걷는 것도 좋아했다

그것을 나만의 해소법이라 해두자

누구나 다 그렇듯이 내 생도 많은 일이 있었고
인생의 가을 3막에 도착한 듯하다

30대에서 40대 초까지의 교수 생활
40대에서 60대까지 20년 이상 하슬라아트월드를 만들어가는 삶
65세인 지금 내가 인생 3막에서 하는 새로운 일

나의 삶은 내 작품과 연결된 이어지는 일이고
아직 끝나지 않았다

나는 종교 철학 역사적 유물들에서 영감을 받으며 작업을 했다
그 대표적 나의 작업 주제가 거울 시리즈였는데
사찰 박물관에서 만난 업경이라는 유물과의 만남 때문이었고
그 외에도 금박시리즈는 적멸보궁 벽의 금박과
유럽 가톨릭 성물의 금박에서 영감을 받았다

경주에서 자란 어린 시절 내내
시내 곳곳에 흩어져 있던 무덤들은
늘 우리 생활과 함께하고 있었다

그것들은 굳이 언어로 표현하자면
생성과 소멸 이음이라는 주제가 되어
지금 나의 예술 속에 스며들었다

그 흔적들
염원이 묻은 것들에게서
지금도 힘을 얻어 살아가고 있다

내 영감의 원천이자 원동력이 된 아름다운 장소
경주와 강릉에 감사를 전한다

그리고 지금은 훌쩍 커버린 세 아이들에게 이글을 바친다

Epilogue

This story was not written chronologically.
The episodes are presented regardless of the flow of time.
It is as if a person with memory loss is trying to recover her memory.

There is no right order to follow.
I thought this would help the reader to experience both space and time together.

To write about the past time... How much of that time could a writer recover?

Perhaps all that past time would be looking at me outside of my writing.

This writing of mine is a meditation on two beautiful places, Gyeongju and Gangneung.
It is also a record of my love and dreams while learning to live in an unfamiliar place, a record of learning things the hard way, which hurt every time but became something to be treasured eventually.

My husband and I were a long-distance couple for 13 years, during which I traveled every week on the coastal road linking the two cities thinking about a lot of things.
For my career as artist, what provided me with inspiration and matrix was the old atmosphere of both cities and their respective natural world and space.

In this personal journey of mine I often struggled with my conflicted feelings, rejections and acceptances, and search for clarity.
That path of mine was always telling me lots of stories, and Route 7 in turn was listening to my stories during my long drive from Gyeongju to Gangneung all those years.

This is something I kept putting off though I had vowed to
begin at the earliest opportunity.
I observe myself moving so slow like a sloth.

I am slow and thinking too much, and I've never been free of
all these things:
the family, schooling, social norms, other people's eyes,
success, things that kept me tied down.

Because I thought my ideal would be elsewhere, I always felt
awkward meeting people socially.
What I preferred instead were
working on a piece of sculpture by myself, sitting for hours in
a favorite space of mine, and walking on a mountain path
without minding the distance.
I also liked walking through the meadow or the city.
Let us say this was my own way of letting out steam.

Like everyone else I've had my own share of experiences,
and I feel I now face my third act, the autumn of my life.

First Act: being a professor in my thirties (until my early
forties),
Second Act: creating Haslla Art World between my forties
and sixties,
Third Act: at age 65 planning something new for the rest of
my life.

My life is a path linked with my artistic work, which is not
over yet.

My work has been inspired by religious, philosophical, and historical artifacts.
One of the representative examples is the mirror series, which came about after my encounter with a Karma mirror at a Buddhist temple museum.
In addition, my gold leaf series was inspired by the gold leaf wall of the sarira shrine in
Sangwonsa and by some of the gold leaf relics of the Catholic church in Europe.

Throughout my childhood in Gyeongju the ancient tombs and tumuli scattered around the city were always part of my life.

If I should verbalize this, it would be a circulation of life and death, a theme which has since become part of my work. Those traces touched with human hopes and aspirations still live on in me.

To Gyeongju and Gangneung, two beautiful places that served as the source and driving force of my inspiration, I say thank you.

And I dedicate this book to my three children who are now grown-ups all of a sudden.

이 책을 만들 때 도움주신 분들께 감사드립니다.

경주에서 강릉까지
from gyeongju to gangneung

발행일	2025. 8. 31
발행인	박신정
발행처	하슬라아트월드
번역	홍진휘
사진	이재중, 황규백
자문	이재중
디자인	김정래, 정혜원

Publication Date	2025. 8. 31
Publisher	Park, Shinjung
Publish	Haslla Art World
Translation	Hong, Jinwhi
Photography	Lee, Jaejung	Hwang, Gyubeak
Advisory	Lee, Jaejung
Design	Kim, Jeongrae	Jeong, Hyewon

이 책에 실린 내용의 무단 전재와 무단 복제를 금합니다.
ⓒ 하슬라아트월드

Unauthorized reproduction or duplication of any part of this book's contents is prohibited.
ⓒ Haslla Art World

The author's Statement

I live and work along the path that runs through the eastern coast of Korea, beside the East Sea.

This road is said by historians and cultural anthropologists to be the final stretch of the ancient Silk Road—tracing a journey that began in Siberia and ended in Korea.

My deep interest in inherited thoughts and visual languages stems from my hometown, Gyeongju, a city built upon the ruins of the thousand-year-old Silla palace.

Even as I studied contemporary art, I felt my identity as an artist was rooted in these origins.

I understand that humanity's beliefs and philosophies about the infinite have evolved into visual forms, becoming archetypes shaped by the history of the Korean people and the natural world that surrounds them.

The author is a graduate of Ewha Womans University, where she completed her undergraduate and graduate studies in fine arts. In 2001 she quit her 13-year professorial career and decided to devote herself to the creation of Haslla Art World in Jeongdongjin.